I0108331

I AM!

10 TRUTHS TO HELP GIRLS KNOW WHO THEY ARE

By MICHELLIAH MCCRANEY

I AM! 10 Truths to Help Girls Know Who They Are
Copyright © 2016 by Michelliah McCraney

ISBN: 978-0-9981013-1-6

Empyrion Publishing
PO Box 784327
Winter Garden, FL
Info@EmpyrionPublishing.com

Unless otherwise noted, all Scripture quotations are from the New King James Version of the Bible.

Photo Credits:
Cover ~ kennykiernanillustration©123rf.com
Page 14 ~ sergein©123rf.com
Page 20 ~ nanettegrebe©123rf.com
Page 22 ~ miramiska©123rf.com
Page 27 ~ michaeljung©123rf.com, franckito©123rf.com, rocketclips©123rf.com, studiograndouest©123rf.com, rohappy©123rf.com, pat138241©123rf.com

All rights reserved. No part of this book may be reproduced, stored in a retrieval system, or transmitted in any form or by any means - electronic, mechanical, photocopy, recording, or any other, without permission in writing from the author.

Printed in the United States of America

I AM!

EDUCATING! EQUIPPING! EMPOWERING!
GIRLS

Building: *Character and Confidence*

Eliminating: *Identity Crisis, Peer Pressure, and Low Self-Esteem*

Teaching: *Etiquette, Behavior, and Responsibility*

Encouraging: *Self-Respect*

Instilling: *Values*

I AM! Series by Michelliah McCraney:

I AM! EVERY GIRL NEEDS TO KNOW WHO SHE IS
I AM! 10 TRUTHS TO HELP GIRLS KNOW WHO THEY ARE
I AM! FUN AND INTERESTING FACTS ABOUT GIRLS FROM
CHILDHOOD TO ADULTHOOD
and
I AM! ALL-IN-ONE WORKBOOK AND JOURNAL

Ms. McCraney has written a very fun book that will educate, empower and equip girls to embrace their authentic self.

Dr. Rosalind Osgood
Chair, Broward County School Board

*Wow! Where was this book when I was growing up? Not only is this a GREAT tool for my 13-year-old daughter, Tiffany, but **I AM!** definitely grabbing copies for my 25-year-old daughter, Mychaela and each one of my NBA son's daughters as well. The illustrations make it inviting and easy to read and I love that it shows a variety of young ladies that reflect the real world. KUDOS to you Michelliah! Thank you for being such a positive example to females of ALL ages.*

Fatima A. Smith, Mother of 5 stars, including NBA forward Michael Beasley
Business Owner & Mentor

Wow! This is an amazing affirmation of the beauty, strength, and talents of girls! Girls of all nationalities can take from these pages a message of pride that will shape their ascent into womanhood. Michelliah McCraney's passion for mentoring and supporting young women is evident in this three part series. She has developed a great resource for girls of all ages on their way to self-discovery.

Nacole S. Guyton, Ed. S, Curriculum Supervisor

To my daughter: Marquitta
To my granddaughters: Taylor and D'Shari

I love you with all my heart!

May you continue to enjoy the beauty and journey
of being a girl and most of all being YOU!

DEAR READER,

It is impossible to know who you are, unless you know the truth about you.

Being a girl can be challenging, interesting, and lots of fun. But the journey of being a girl can be even better when you understand your strengths and weaknesses; when you know who you truly are.

The first thing I want you to know is regardless of your circumstances, or where you've been or why, you are important to me!

Therefore, I would like for every girl that reads this book to embrace it as your BFF (Best Friend Forever).

As you read this book, you may be hearing some of these things for the first time. I want you to read and re-read until you KNOW that these things are TRUE about YOU!

If, by chance, you've heard more bad things than good things about yourself, don't believe them. I have good news for you. This is your opportunity to embrace what is really true about you!

You are a significant piece of a puzzle that cannot be completed without you.

A Prayer for Every Girl Who Reads this Book:

Heavenly Father, please smile on this young lady.

Let her be empowered by the words You have given me to write in this book.

Help her to see herself through these words. Help her to love herself unconditionally.

Increase her confidence and strengthen her where she may be weak.

Through this book please build her character and fix any low self-esteem issues she may have. Show her what gifts she possesses and everything you intend for her to be.

Tell her who she is, and when she learns who she really is, help her to never forget. Help her to set standards and goals for herself that are achievable and that are not centered on her peers or any young man.

Give her power to say no when necessary and courage to do the right thing when she doesn't feel like it.

If she is hurting or having a hard time in any area of her mind, body or spirit, heal her.

If she is confused or feels neglected, restore her. If she is lost, secure her and bring her to safety. If she needs change, transform her.

If she has ever walked with her head down, been picked on, felt like she doesn't fit in, or been abused, I ask that You make her to walk with her head held high, and cause her to never be afraid of, or bullied by another creature from this day forth.

And lastly, Lord, when she comes to the end and closes this book, I ask that You give her peace and that You would continue to meet her every need.

AMEN

Knowing Who You Are

Knowing who you are is one of the most important things you will accomplish in life. It can also be one of the most interesting discoveries you'll ever make.

And I cannot think of a better person to know than YOU, or a better time than now to begin, while you are yet still young with lots and lots of growing and learning to do.

WHO ARE YOU?

15 Reasons
Why It Is Important for Girls to Know the Truth

Words are powerful!

Words can build you up or tear you down.

Words can make you feel good or make you feel bad.

Words can make you laugh or make you cry.

Words can make you feel strong or make you feel weak.

Words can make you feel happy or make you feel sad.

Words can empower you or break you.

Words become thoughts.

Words become actions.

Words become beliefs.

Words produce life.

People can be mean.

People can be dishonest.

People can disappoint (let you down) you.

People can hurt you.

But the truth can set you free!

TRUTH # 1
I AM! IMPORTANT

I was born with and for a purpose.

I was created and designed with a mission in mind; there is a plan and destiny that is all mine. It has already been written with my name attached to it and underlined. Here's a little bit of how it is defined:

I am here to do great things. I am here to serve. I am here to make a difference somewhere and somehow. These things will be accomplished through my ideas, ambitions, and aspirations, as they are sure to come in time.

I have the ability to become the next Michelle Obama or Oprah Winfrey, or the first to complete high school or obtain a college degree within my family.

- ❖ I was born on the day, date, and in the month I was born on purpose.

- ❖ I was given the name I have on purpose.

- ❖ I was born or placed into the family and given the parents or guardians I have for a reason.

- ❖ I am the color I am on purpose.

- ❖ I speak the language I do for a reason.

- ❖ I possess the gift(s) I do on purpose.

I could have been an animal, tree, car or any other type of thing that exists on earth. Instead, I was given power over all creation at birth. There are scriptures in the Bible that prove my worth (see Genesis 1:26 and Matthew 6:26)

What I do with my time here on earth matters. It matters to me and it matters to others. Unless you are a significant piece of that puzzle, your opinion about me or my future is unimportant.

My name is _____ and I AM Important!

TRUTH #2
I AM! SMART

❖   I go to school to learn.

❖   I accept that school is my job and my grades are my pay. So I must work hard to earn good grades.

❖   Getting an education and one day graduating from high school is not an option for me, but a goal and a requirement.

- ❖ I am not dumb. I have the ability to learn new things.

- ❖ I can learn what appears to be hard or difficult.

- ❖ I use the resources around me, like my parents or guardians, teachers, pastor, or school counselor, to advise me instead of listening to my peers or leaning on my own understanding.

- ❖ I involve myself in extracurricular activities afterschool and outside of school to gain skills that will help me to express my talents and develop my social skills.

- ❖ I consider being a part of things that can one day possibly earn me a scholarship to college.

- ❖ I listen to positive music, with a positive message.

- ❖ I read books, magazines, and the newspaper.

- ❖ I listen to the news to learn about current events that are going on in the world, and I sometimes even research things on the internet.

- ❖ I study and practice to become good at a particular subject.

- ❖ I know that no question is a dumb question.

- ❖ I accept that making straight A's in school doesn't mean I know everything or am smarter than everyone else.

- ❖ I humble myself to learn from others that are older and wiser than me, as well as others who are younger, because they too can be helpful.

- ❖ I make plans and set goals that are reasonable and that I can accomplish.

- ❖ I will one day go to college, choose a career or own my own business, and work to earn my own money.

My name is _____ and I AM Smart!

TRUTH #3
I AM! BEAUTIFUL

I AM an image of God (see Genesis 1:26).

I am a beautiful creation, handmade by God. When He was done putting me together and adding all of the finishing touches, He stood back, took one last look, and was happy with me. I know this because in the Bible, Genesis 1:31 says, "Then God looked over all He had made, and He saw it was very good."

Beauty can be found in a color, shape, or size. It is a personal preference in our own eyes.

I have special characteristics that help to make me look beautiful…like the color of my skin, facial features, hair texture, height, the curves of my body, and my smile.

Yet, there is another huge hidden characteristic that everyone cannot physically see. But if they listen and pay close attention, they will be able to know.

It is my HEART; it is the one that lives on the inside of me. It is where the work is done that makes me a better me. That is why:

- ❖ My clothes don't make me. I make the clothes. What I wear looks good simply because of me.

- ❖ My shoes don't make me. I make the shoes. It is how I walk in the shoes that cause them to stand out.

- ❖ My hair style doesn't make me. I make it. My hair complements the expression of beauty that springs from my skin tone, shines from my eyes, and curves along the defined shape of my nose and lips.

My beauty is natural and that's what makes me all that and a bag of chips.

I guess that is why I am "It." For in beauty, only, do I exist!

My name is _____ and I AM Beautiful!

TRUTH #4
I AM! UNIQUE

The best part about being unique is that you get to be you, and I get to be me. This simply means there is no reason to compete.

Being unique means being different and celebrating your own gifts and qualities that make you stand out from everyone else.

I am unique because I am an audience of one. This means:

- ❖ I am not a copycat, or mimic of anyone.
- ❖ I don't dress like, act like, talk like, or try to look or be like everybody else or any one particular person.
- ❖ I don't try to keep up with the latest trends, like all the name brand clothing and shoes or the popular people in school.
- ❖ I shop to buy and wear what I like and what I think looks good on me.
- ❖ I have my own mind, style, and way of doing things.
- ❖ I am comfortable in my own skin.
- ❖ I am not a member of any gang, or clique. I'm not in need of a dress code, slogan, or gang sign to define who I am.

You see, unique things are priceless because of the time, work, and energy put into creating them. Yet, there are a couple of other things that go along with being unique:

- ❖ I am sometimes judged, labeled or misunderstood.
- ❖ I am also called names like weird, strange, special or queer.

I think this is because many of my peers are afraid to be themselves so they copy and name call out of fear.

I am an ORIGINAL, AUTHENTIC work of art and for the rest of my life, this is the brand I will ROCK!

My name is _____ and I AM Unique!

TRUTH #5
I AM! CONFIDENT

We need confidence in God, just as much as we need to have confidence in ourselves and our abilities.

Hebrews 10:35 in the Bible, tells us not to throw away our confidence; it will be richly rewarded. That is why:

- ❖ I do not doubt or second-guess myself because I am sure about me.

- ❖ I am not jealous, envious, or fearful of anyone.

- ❖ I am bold and fearless.

- ❖ I have the courage to go after what I want and believe I can have.

- ❖ I believe in myself and my abilities even when no one else does.

- ❖ I believe that I can be anything I aspire to be.

- ❖ I don't speak "I can't," or think "I can't," or believe "I can't." All of my sentences begin with "I can and I will because I believe I can!"

- ❖ Being confident is being humble and not arrogant, conceited, or prideful.

- ❖ It is not an act, but an assurance of who I AM and what I AM capable of creating, having or owning.

- ❖ Some people say that the sky is the limit to what we can have. In my opinion this means that I can go as high as I can imagine, do as much as I am willing, and take as much as I can bear.

- ❖ My confidence tells me that I can do it! But my faith in God tells me that it is already done, even when I can't actually see it yet.

My name is _____ and I AM Confident!

TRUTH #6
I AM! RESPONSIBLE

- ❖ I finish what I start.
- ❖ No one has to make me study, do my homework, or complete my chores.
- ❖ I can be trusted to go where I am supposed to and come right back.
- ❖ I get to school and class on time.
- ❖ I am able to keep up with my personal or valuable belongings.
- ❖ I am capable of grooming myself and maintaining my personal hygiene. I can prepare (wash, iron) my clothing (uniform) for school the night before and dress myself appropriately.
- ❖ I can handle staying at home alone. I know to lock the doors and not open the door for strangers or make it known that I am home alone.
- ❖ I turn off important things after using them like the stove, iron, water and lights.
- ❖ I am capable of getting a permission slip from school to my parent or guardian and returning it to my teacher signed the next day, as instructed.
- ❖ I can properly communicate a message. I am dependable, trustworthy, and accountable.
- ❖ I can be sent to the store to purchase household items or groceries and bring back the appropriate amount of change.
- ❖ I do not give in to negative peer pressure to hang out, smoke, skip school, drink alcohol, or use drugs because my peers think it is cool or because everyone else is doing it.
- ❖ I do not allow boys or my peers to talk me into doing things I shouldn't be doing until I am older, more educated, ready or married.
- ❖ If I make plans to go to the library to study with some friends to prepare for a test, but they decide to do something else, I don't deviate (get side tracked) from that plan. I simply tell them that I will catch up with them later and stick to what is a priority to me.
- ❖ I accept that as I grow older, so will my responsibilities and others' expectations of me.

My name is _____ and I AM Responsible!

TRUTH #7
I AM! SECURE

- ❖ I don't compare myself to others.
- ❖ I don't give in to negative things others may think or say about me.
- ❖ I know what I want and like, and I do not settle for less.
- ❖ I don't allow others to determine how I am going to act or react.
- ❖ I don't try to fit in where I am not wanted or welcomed.
- ❖ I use my options.
- ❖ I am not ashamed of my family, what we have or don't have, or what we can or cannot afford.
- ❖ I am proud of who I am and where I am from.
- ❖ I don't pretend to be someone I am not or to have something I do not have.
- ❖ I strongly believe that what's for me is for me and can't anyone prevent me from having it.
- ❖ I walk with my head held high, sit with my back straight, and when I am speaking to others, I am not afraid to look them in the eyes.
- ❖ I do not see anyone as being better than me.
- ❖ I don't have to make myself feel as though I am better than anyone else.
- ❖ I don't make up stories about where I am going or where I have been to make it seem as if I've got it going on.
- ❖ I am not afraid to speak or stand up for myself when I know that I am right.
- ❖ I am not easily offended.
- ❖ I am not easily broken. When people say or do things to hurt me, I may bend, but I will not break.

My name is _____ and I AM Secure!

TRUTH #8
I AM! VICTORIOUS

I am more than a child of the King. I am a sister of a King's kid.

- ❖ I possess some of the same characteristics within me that are in Him.
- ❖ I may be small or one to an army of five, but with God on my side, I don't have to ever be afraid of giants (bullies).
- ❖ I am a winner and not a loser.
- ❖ I AM NOT my failures, hurts, or disappointments. I am a winner that stands victoriously as a result of them.
- ❖ I have a victorious mind, body and spirit. I think, see, smell and taste victory.
- ❖ I have a winning attitude. I leave vengeance (payback) to God.
- ❖ I rejoice in the mist of trouble because I know that it won't last forever, and it will only make me stronger. And because I believe victory is upon me, I will not be defeated.
- ❖ I refuse to let where I've been or what I've been through determine my future.
- ❖ I am not a victim. I AM a Victor!
- ❖ Like David in the bible who one day had to face his giant, Goliath, I will too! And when I do, I believe just like David that I, too, will come out victorious.

David killed his giant with a stone and a sling. You can read about it in 1Samuel 17:48-51.

But not every victory will be won like this. Some victories are won after a long, hard fight. This is what makes our victories worth celebrating.

My name is _____ and I AM Victorious!

TRUTH #9
I AM! ETIQUETTE

- ❖ I use words like, "Thank you," "No, thank you," "You're welcome," "Please," "May I," and even, "Excuse me" or "Pardon me."

- ❖ I don't talk when others are talking.

- ❖ When I meet people for the first time, I smile, offer a handshake and introduce myself.

- ❖ I bless the food before eating.

- ❖ I place a napkin in my lap before I eat to protect my clothing. It helps to catch any food or spills that may occur.

- ❖ I eat with my utensils (fork, spoon, knife), and not my hands.

- ❖ I don't talk with my mouth full or chew with my mouth open.

- ❖ I don't lick my fingers when eating. I don't clean my mouth with my tongue, hands or any part of my clothing. Instead, I use a napkin to wipe my mouth.

- ❖ I do not eat with my elbows on the table, nor do I sit in a slouched position. Instead, I sit with my back straight, using good posture, with my arms under the table.

- ❖ I cover my mouth when I cough so I do not cough on others. I cover my mouth and excuse myself when I burp, but if I am able to avoid this, I do.

- ❖ I turn my head away from others when I sneeze, or sneeze into my arm and not my hands so I do not spread germs.

- ❖ When I am at a restaurant and I am done eating, I place my fork in a downward position next to my knife or resting over it to let the server know that I am finished.

- ❖ I don't reach across another person at the table to get food or something I need. Instead, I ask them to please pass the dish or utensils to me.

❖ In formal settings such as weddings, special dinner parties, or other occasions, I notice the setting of the table so that I use the appropriate utensils.

❖ I have great table manners and class.

❖ If I am being accompanied by a gentleman to an event and he desires to assist me as I take my seat, I stand back and provide enough space for him to pull out my chair for me. Then I step in front of the chair and wait for him to push it in. Once the chair is in position, I take my seat and slightly turn my head toward him, smile, and say, "Thank you."

❖ If that gentleman should ask me for a dance, I offer (give) him my hand and allow him to lead me to the dance floor.

My name is _____ and I AM Etiquette!

TRUTH #10
I AM! A CLASS ACT

- ❖ I treat others how I desire to be treated.
- ❖ I don't lie, cheat, or steal from others.
- ❖ I make moral choices, not popular choices.
- ❖ I am able to say "yes" to what is right and "no" to what is wrong.
- ❖ I am empowered to lead and not follow.
- ❖ I don't follow the crowd. If there's a fight in school, I don't run to it. Instead, I walk away from it.
- ❖ I refuse to participate in picking on or making fun of others.
- ❖ When someone chooses to be the class clown and constantly disrupt the classroom environment, I don't jump on the band wagon (become a part). I don't support such behavior or actions by laughing at it or mimicking what they are doing.
- ❖ I spend quality time on school projects, writing assignments, such as essays and even my homework. Presentation (looks, arrangement, and design) is important to me.
- ❖ I choose my friends, company, and words wisely.
- ❖ I carefully choose the places I go and the people I go with.
- ❖ I choose my battles. I don't argue, fuss, or fight over every little thing. Yet, I understand that I may not be able to always avoid conflict (disagreement).
- ❖ I know how to ignore, walk away, and be the bigger person.
- ❖ I do not have to have the last word.
- ❖ I can express and defend myself or get my point across without the use of profanity.
- ❖ Keeping a good reputation is everything to me.

I am an exceptional girl; not just any girl. Exceptional means: unusual, remarkable, extraordinary, abnormal, rare, special and phenomenal. Exceptional equals ME! My name is _____ and I AM A Class Act!

THE REAL TRUTH IS...ALL GIRLS ROCK!
(Every Color, Age, Look, Size or Shape)

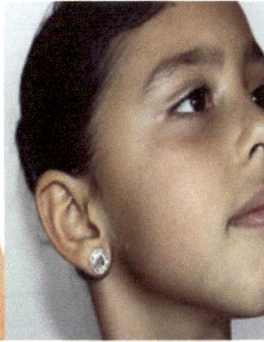

I AM! MICHELLIAH McCRANEY
the author of this book...

...and "I Rock!"

Because inside of me arc bits and pieces of YOU.

THE END!

Michelliah McCraney is a mother, grandmother, educator, mentor, inspirational speaker, and spoken word artist. She is also the Founder and Executive Director of Aspiring Beautiful & Confident Girls, Inc.

Ms. McCraney was born and raised in South Florida. She has worked in Florida's public school system in Miami-Dade, Broward and Alachua county using her skills to enhance the lives of children and families in need.

Throughout her 21-year tenure, Ms. McCraney has worked with Head Start, Pre-K and elementary school children. The children she has worked with include Exceptional Student Education (ESE), Attention Deficit Hyperactivity Disorder (ADHD), Attention Deficit Disorder (ADD) and those diagnosed with Autism Spectrum Disorder (ASD). As a Behavior Research Teacher (BRT), she successfully transformed the behavior of many challenging students.

Advancing in her career, Ms. McCraney administered the Parent Resource Center and various after school programs, arranged Career Day programs, organized Youth Mentoring Programs, and implemented Parenting Workshops. In addition, she built partnerships with local businesses throughout the community to support incentive programs for students and families in need.

Embracing her gifts, Ms. McCraney wrote and produced her first Poetry CD in 2010, after which she carried out her vision of writing and publishing her very own curriculum to mentor and teach young girls.

Accepting her purpose, what was only intended to be one book became a three-part series with a matching journal.

www.ingramcontent.com/pod-product-compliance
Lightning Source LLC
Chambersburg PA
CBHW041551040426
42447CB00002B/137

9 780998 101316